a gift for

_____

from

_____

WIT & WISDOM

of

WOMEN

Classic and Contemporary Quotes

BOK2071

The Wit and Wisdom of Women: Classic and Contemporary Quotes

Copyright © 2006
Hallmark Licensing, Inc.
ISBN: 1-59530-126-7

Published by Gift Books from Hallmark, a division of Hallmark Cards, Inc.
Kansas City, MO 64141

Visit us on the Web at www.Hallmark.com.

Art Director: Kevin Swanson
Editorial Director: Todd Hafer

Editorial development by SnapdragonGroup[SM] Editorial Services
Designed by: Craig Bissell

Printed and bound in China.

WIT & WISDOM

of

WOMEN

Classic and Contemporary Quotes

TABLE *of* CONTENTS

INTRODUCTION

$\mathcal{I}$f you think it's a man's world out there, honey,
you haven't been paying attention. Every day we are
surrounded by women who inspire us with their kindness,
wit, and courage. They are our sisters, our mothers,
our best friends and co-workers — and sometimes even
strangers. They make us laugh, let us cry, push us forward,
and watch our backs. Some inspire the whole country,
while others become our closest friends.

No matter who she is, each woman brings a special touch
that no other person has. Her impact on others is nothing
short of profound. The quotes in this book not only celebrate
her special way of connecting with others but also remind us
of the wise, funny, loving person she is: In a tough world,
she is tender. In a big world, she is fearless. In ever-changing
times, she is a constant friend — and a woman like that
makes all the difference in the world.

THE MYSTERIES OF MEN, MARRIAGE, AND ROMANCE

Love is like playing checkers.
You have to know which man to move.

Moms Mabley

One of the most important things about a man is
that he should be kind—
kind of tall...
kind of handsome...
kind of rich...

Mary Ellen Lowe

A woman's got to love a bad man once or twice in her life
to be thankful for a good one.

Marjorie Kinnan Rawlings

I've heard that dogs are man's best friend.
That explains where men are getting their hygiene tips.

Kelly Maguire

We're still our own worst enemies a lot of the time,
but I still blame men.

Janeane Garofalo

If the world's so fair...
how come men don't have P.M.S.?

Linda Elrod

I want my husband to take me in his arms and whisper
those three little words that all women long to hear:
"You were right."

Kelly Smith

Men: If you can't beat 'em,
cut 'em off from sex.

Dee Ann Stewart

The only way to have really safe sex is to abstain.
From drinking.

Wendy Liebman

People want to take sex education out of the schools.
They believe sex education causes promiscuity.
Hey, I took algebra. I never do math.

Elayne Boosler

When you've got the personality, you don't need the nudity.

Mae West

I'm a modern woman;
most of my fantasies are of more sleep.

Laura Hayden

Women might be able to fake orgasms.
But men can fake entire relationships.

Sharon Stone

Plain women know more about men than beautiful ones do.

Katharine Hepburn

Can you imagine a world without men?
No crime and lots of fat, happy women.

Nicole Hollander

When a man brings his wife flowers for no reason,
there's a reason.

Molly McGee

Macho does not prove mucho.

Zsa Zsa Gabor

Why do women go to tanning salons?
What a waste of time and money.
Guys only like the white parts anyway.

Margot Black

A fool and her money are soon courted.

Helen Rowland

Money does not change men; it only unmasks them.

Marie-Jeanne Riccoboni

Just remember,
a fool and his money...
are always better than no date at all.

Allyson Jones

The best way to get most husbands to do something
is to suggest that perhaps they're too old to do it.

Shirley MacLaine

Love is like pi – natural, irrational, and very important.

Lisa Hoffman

Give a man a fish and he eats for a day.
Teach him how to fish and you get rid of him
for the whole weekend.

Zenna Schaffer

I'd like to have a boyfriend in prison
so I'd always know where he was.

Carrie Snow

Dr. Ruth says women should tell our lovers how to make love to us.
My boyfriend goes nuts if I tell him how to drive.

Pam Stone

Men do cry, but only when assembling furniture.

Rita Rudner

You can fool some people some of the time...
and men pretty much all the time.

Dee Ann Stewart

If they can send a man to the moon...
why can't they send ALL of them to the moon?

Dorothy Colgan

If love means never having to say you're sorry,
then marriage means always having to say everything twice.

Estelle Getty

A bride at a second wedding does not wear a veil.
She wants to see what she is getting.

Helen Rowland

Keep in mind that no matter how cute and sexy a guy is,
there's always some woman somewhere who is sick of him.

Carol Henry

A kiss is a lovely trick designed by nature
to stop speech when words become superfluous.

Ingrid Bergman

Sometimes it seems that all the really good-looking,
together, sensitive men are taken —
by other really good-looking, together, sensitive men.

Allyson Jones

They say women love a man in uniform. It's true.
The uniform sends a clear message: He has a job.

Mimi Gonzalez

You won't get a man to do what you want by dressing sexy.
If you want a man to listen to you, dress like his mother.

Dianna Jordan

I've been on so many blind dates that I should get a free dog.

Wendy Liebman

Before I met my husband, I'd never fallen in love —
though I'd stepped in it a few times.

Rita Rudner

I think; therefore, I'm single.

Lizz Winstead

It's not the men in your life that counts,
it's the life in your men.

Mae West
(as Tira in *I'm No Angel*, 1933)

Today's women are not only beautiful, but also confident,
intelligent, independent, and savvy —
Do today's men deserve us?

Trish Berrong

Nothing turns a man's head like a pot roast!
A tender, juicy cut of beef laden with baby carrots julienne
and cubed new potatoes will keep a satisfied grin
on his face for hours!
Serving it naked helps, as well.

Dee Ann Stewart

The ultimate test of a relationship is to disagree but to hold hands.

Alexandra Penney

INSPIRING WORDS FROM INSPIRING WOMEN

Alone we can do so little; together we can do so much.

Helen Keller

If I can stop one heart from breaking, I shall not live in vain.

Emily Dickinson

No one can make you feel inferior without your consent.

Eleanor Roosevelt

Love liberates everything.

Maya Angelou

The hunger for love is more difficult to feed
than the hunger for bread.

Mother Teresa

Never lose your zeal for building a better world.

Mary McLeod Bethune

Action is the antidote to despair.

Joan Baez

If you can't do it with feeling, don't.

Patsy Cline

People who fight fire with fire usually end up with ashes.

Abigail Van Buren

Good manners will often take people where neither money
nor education will take them.

Fanny Jackson Coppin

Ideas are a dime a dozen.
People who implement them are priceless.

Mary Kay Ash

To be content with little is hard;
to be content with much is impossible.

Marie Ebner-Eschenbach

The heart outgrows old grief.

Ella Wheeler-Wilcox

A woman who loves always has success.

Vicki Baum

Love lights more fires than hate can extinguish.

Ella Wheeler-Wilcox

If your experiences would benefit anybody,
give them to someone.

Florence Nightingale

Kind words can be short and easy to speak,
but their echoes are truly endless.

Mother Teresa

It is better to light a candle than to curse the darkness.

Eleanor Roosevelt

Service is the rent you pay for room on this earth.

Shirley Chisholm

It's not the load that breaks you down;
it's the way you carry it.

Lena Horne

A woman is like a tea bag.
You never know how strong she is
until she gets into hot water.

Eleanor Roosevelt

Duty takes us to places we never expected;
love brings us home.

Sarah Mueller

I am a woman above everything else.

Jacqueline Kennedy Onassis

Goals are dreams with deadlines.

Diana Scharf Hunt

Courage is fear that has said its prayers.

Dorothy Bernard

Your passion is waiting for your courage to catch up.

Marilyn Greist

Give curiosity freedom.

Eudora Welty

Defeat in this world is no disgrace,
if you really fought for the right thing.

Katherine Ann Porter

Mistakes are a fact of life.
It's the response to the error that counts.

Nikki Giovanni

Wisdom means not making the same mistakes
over and over again.

Jessica Tandy

Don't ever mind being called tough.
Be strong and have definite ideas and opinions.

Rosalynn Carter

You learn by going where you have to go.

Mia Farrow

It doesn't matter if it takes a long time getting there;
the point is to have a destination.

Eudora Welty

If we forget our past, we won't remember our future,
because we won't have one.

Flannery O'Connor

It isn't where you come from;
it's where you're going that counts.

Ella Fitzgerald

You've got to continue to grow, or you're just like last night's cornbread – stale and dry.

Loretta Lynn

What is very difficult at first, if we keep on trying,
gradually becomes easier.

Helen Keller

When I stand before God at the end of my life, I would hope
that I would not have a single bit of talent left and could say:
I used everything you gave me.

Erma Bombeck

Success and failure are greatly overrated.
But failure gives you a whole lot more to talk about.

Hildegaard Knef

We are not here to be successful. We are here to be faithful.

Mother Teresa

The more I wonder, the more I love.

Alice Walker

You may have to fight a battle more than once to win it.

Margaret Thatcher

We may encounter many defeats, but we must not be defeated.

Maya Angelou

We can learn to love only by loving.

Iris Murdoch

Be happy. It's one way of being wise.

Colette

AGING WITH
(OR WITHOUT) GRACE

Sex appeal is 50 percent what you've got
and 50 percent what people think you've got.

Sophia Loren

It's not how old you are but how you are old.

Marie Dressler

Whatever wrinkles I got, I enjoyed getting them.

Ava Gardner

I refuse to admit that I am more than fifty-two,
even if that does make my sons illegitimate.

Nancy Astor

Another belief of mine: that everyone else my age is an adult, whereas I am merely in disguise.

Margaret Atwood

I'd like to grow very old as slowly as possible.

Irene Mayer Selznick

If women were meant to age gracefully,
God wouldn't have created little red convertibles.

Linda Staten

Age is all imagination. Ignore years, and they'll ignore you.

Ella Wheeler-Wilcox

In youth we learn. In age we understand.

Marie Ebner-Eschenbach

Surely the consolation of old age is finding out how few things
are worth worrying over.

Dorothy Dix

Though it sounds absurd, it is true to say that I
felt younger at sixty than I felt at twenty.

Ellen Glasgow

Do not deprive me of my age. I have earned it.

May Sarton

Inside every older person is a younger person —
wondering what the hell happened.

Cora Harvey Armstrong

Old age is no place for sissies.

Bette Davis

So much has been said and sung of the beautiful young girls.
Why don't somebody wake up to the beauty of old women?

Harriet Beecher Stowe

ON HEALTH, DIETS, AND FITNESS...

The first time I see a jogger smiling, I'll consider it.

Joan Rivers

THE ABC'S OF HEALTHY, HAPPY LIVING

Act Assertively
Be Brave
Clear out Clutter
Delight in Daisies
Explore Everything
Feed Friendships
Grow Gracefully
Harvest Happiness
Invest in Ice Cream
Jump for Joy
Keep Kissing
Laugh Lots
Make Miracles

Nurture Nature
Opt for Optimism
Praise People
Quit Quibbling
Relax Regularly
Seek Simplicity
Take Time
Use an Umbrella
Value Veggies
Welcome Wisdom
Xceed Xpectations
Yell Yes
ZZzzzzzzz's (Get plenty of 'em!)

Cheryl Hawkinson

The secret to staying young is to live honestly,
eat slowly, and lie about your age.

Lucille Ball

My favorite machine at the gym is the vending machine.

Caroline Rhea

I always keep three sizes of clothes in my closet...
"normal days,"
"bloated days,"
and "those were the days."

Myra Zirkle

If God meant for us to be naked,
he would have made our skin fit better.

Maureen Murphy

No day is so bad that it can't be fixed with a nap.

Carrie Snow

Men date thin girls because they're too weak to argue —
and salads are cheap.

Jennifer Fairbanks

Careful grooming may take twenty years off a woman's age,
but you can't fool a long flight of stairs.

Marlene Dietrich

Everything you see, I owe to spaghetti.

Sophia Loren

Helpful Diet Tip:
Rice cakes taste better dipped in hot fudge.

Allyson Jones

Man cannot live by chocolate alone.
(But women can.)

Dee Ann Stewart

The process of trying on bathing suits
is just nature's little way of keeping us humble.
Very humble.

Cheryl Hawkinson

Some days I feel I have the weight of the world
on my shoulders. Then, other days, I feel like it's on my hips.

Robin St. John

Brain cells come and brain cells go,
but fat cells live forever.

Linda Staten

I'm lazy.
At work my favorite part of the day is being on hold.

Janet Rosen

"Good-bye" is hard to say — not as hard, perhaps, as
"No cheesecake for me, thanks."
But it's hard.

Myra Zirkle

DIET SECRETS ALL WOMEN KNOW:

1. Food is not as fattening if you eat it standing up.
2. If you wait to eat something until you can't stand it any longer, you burn many calories during those moments of courageous self-denial.
3. If you feel guilty enough about eating something, it cancels out the calories.
4. Cookie dough, cake batter, or other uncooked foods do not have nearly the pounds-on potential as the actual end products.
5. Ice cream has fewer calories if you eat it out of the carton.
6. Cutting fattening food into tiny pieces allows many calories to evaporate into the atmosphere
7. You will not gain weight from eating a rich dessert if the dessert actually belongs to someone else.
8. The mere thought of exercise frightens calories away.

Suzanne Heins

ON FAMILY AND FRIENDS...

Every year my family would pile into the car for our vacation
and drive 80 trillion miles just to prove that we couldn't
get along in any setting.

Janeane Garofalo

One thing I've discovered in general about raising kids is that they really don't give a damn if you walked five miles to school.

Patty Duke

In general, my children refuse to eat anything
that hasn't danced on television.

Erma Bombeck

They say kids keep you young.
Of course, so do cosmetics,
and they sleep through the night.

Cheryl Hawkinson

It is a scientific fact that undesirable traits
that show up in children are inherited
from "his" side of the family.

Bobbie Burrow

One of the luckiest things that can happen to you in life
is to have a happy childhood.

Agatha Christie

In the end, it's not what you do for your children
but what you've taught them to do for themselves.

Ann Landers

My grandmother used to can vegetables for her family.
My mom used to bake home-made cookies.
I sometimes let the kids choose which drive-thru we go to.
The circle of love continues.

Mary Ellen Lowe

Any mother could perform the jobs of several
air-traffic controllers with great ease.

Lisa Alther

When I'm in a store and I see a little girl
wearing a tutu and a cowboy hat, I think,
There's a mom who lost an argument.

Dee Ann Stewart

"Do you want to go to bed early?"
"Do you need a spanking?"
"Are you looking to get grounded?"
Moms — the great masters of the rhetorical question.

Tina Neidlein

You wouldn't think the miracle of life would involve wearing big giant underpants... but there you are.

Jennifer Fujita

You know you're a mother when...
You find yourself humming "I'm a Little Teapot"
for no apparent reason.
You tune in to Saturday-morning cartoons
even though the kids aren't home.
You visit a friend after major surgery and offer to
"kiss the boo-boo and make it better."
You automatically say "Look both ways" when you cross the street,
even if you're alone.
You justify all decisions with the simple phrase,
"Because I said so; that's why!"
You're on a first-name basis with the ice-cream-truck driver.
You cut other adults' entrees into bite-sized portions.

Molly Wigand

EVERY MOTHER KNOWS...

...all children are little angels...especially when asleep!

...the three most dreaded words in the English language are: NO SCHOOL TODAY!

...there are three ways to get kids to eat what's good for them:
   a. Cover it with catsup
   b. Serve it over ice cream
   c. Tell them they can't have it

...children like two kinds of clothing: ugly and expensive.

...just because kids can sing every word to every song on the Top Forty doesn't mean they can learn a four-line poem for the school play.

...if God had meant for families to eat together, He wouldn't have created after-school activities.

AND...no matter how action-packed and perplexing life with children can be...being a mom is really the most rewarding job of all!

Mary Ellen Lowe

Constant use will not wear ragged the fabric of friendship.

Dorothy Parker

A foreigner is a friend I've yet to meet.

Pearl Buck

A TRUE FRIEND IS...

1. someone who will keep your secrets and never divulge them — even if tortured or tempted with chocolate.

2. the person who will quietly destroy the photograph that makes you look like a beached whale.

3. the person who will also destroy the negative of the photograph that makes you look like a beached whale.

4. someone who knows that sometimes you don't know what you're talking about, but will let you reach that conclusion independently.

5. a person who will go on the same diet with you — and off it, too.

6. someone who knows you're fibbing if you say "Everything's fine," when it's really not.

7. the person who can tell you that you have a green vegetable between your front teeth and can do it without making you feel like a social reject.

8. the person who'll tell you that the outfit the salesclerk just told you was "you" is definitely "somebody else."

9. someone who laughs at the same jokes, cries at the same movies, and shares your weakness for chocolate.

Robin St. John

A real friend
knows when to listen,
when to stop listening,
when to talk,
when to stop talking,
when to pour wine,
and when to stop pouring
and just hand over the bottle.

Lee Franklin

There is no problem
that two friends cannot
ignore,
discuss,
plot against,
make fun of,
or drown in chocolate sauce.

Jennifer Fujita

Men come and go, but friends are forever.
And they're really handy at mocking the men who go.

Robin St. John

Women don't just have friends.
We have soulmates...
and that is powerful compensation
for life's other hardships.

Alarie Tennille

So many of my favorite stories begin with
"One time, my sister and I..."

Tina Neidlein

A sister is a friend who shares your
troublesome thigh problem.

Lee Franklin

Your sister helped make you what you are today —
loyal and protective of your jewelry.

Allyson Jones

QUOTABLE QUIPS

What the world really needs is more love and less paperwork.

Pearl Bailey

All we want is peace on earth...
and really cute shoes.

Allyson Jones

Some days every woman you meet has the hair you want.

Dee Ann Stewart

I always wanted to be somebody,
but I should have been more specific.

Lily Tomlin

Boys will be boys.
Girls will be women.

Amie Doyen

You can't keep a good woman down.

Alice Walker

The truth will set you free. But first, it will piss you off.

Gloria Steinem

I'm in therapy now. I used to be in denial.
Which is a lot cheaper.

Robin Greenspan

In real life, I assure you, there is no such thing as algebra.

Fran Lebowitz

I don't call it gossip; I call it "emotional speculation."

Laurie Colwin

I call everyone "darling," because I can't remember their names.

Zsa Zsa Gabor

Remember, if people talk behind your back,
it only means you are two steps ahead.

Fannie Flagg

Knowledge is power, if you know it about the right person.

Ethel Watts Mumford

People who drink to drown their sorrows should be told that sorrow knows how to swim.

Ann Landers

Art is the only way to run away without leaving home.

Twyla Tharp

Bite off more than you can chew,
then chew it.

Ella Williams

God has a plan for all of us, but He expects us to do
our share of the work.

Minnie Pearl

Everyone has talent. What is rare is the courage to
follow that talent wherever it leads.

Erica Jong

Don't compromise yourself.
You're all you've got.

Janis Joplin

My license plate says PMS.
Nobody cuts me off.

Wendy Liebman

If you love something, set it free.
Unless it's chocolate.
Never release chocolate.

Renee Duvall

When life gets too hectic, I've always found that
a nice, hot bath can solve most problems...
For everything else, there's denial.

Keely Chace

Fashion can be bought. Style one must possess.

Edna Woolman

I'm not offended by all the dumb blonde jokes because
I know that I'm not dumb...and I also know that I'm not blonde.

Dolly Parton

I love to sleep. It's the best of both worlds.
You get to be alive, and unconscious.

Rita Rudner

If it won't catch fire today, clean it tomorrow.

Erma Bombeck

Inside every woman is a feisty little girl
who wants to jump and dance and blow bubbles,
and who is absolutely NOT interested
in balancing a checkbook.

Cheryl Hawkinson

I think I'm a pretty good judge of people,
which is why I hate most of them.

Roseanne Barr

Juries scare me. I don't want to put my fate in the hands of twelve people who couldn't get out of jury duty.

Monica Piper

It's better to light just one candle than to clean the whole apartment.

Eileen Courtney

Procrastination gives you something to look forward to.

Joan Konner

I'm extraordinarily patient,
provided I get my own way in the end.

Margaret Thatcher

Reality is the leading cause of stress for those in touch with it.

Jane Wagner

A person who talks fast often says things she hasn't thought of yet.

Caron Warner Lieber

"Excuse my dust."

Dorothy Parker's self-chosen epitaph

Speak the truth — no matter what comes of it.

Ellen Glasgow

The next best thing to being clever
is being able to quote someone who is.

Mary Pettibone Poole

If you have enjoyed this book
or it has touched your life in some way,
Hallmark would love to hear from you.

Please send your comments to:
Book Feedback
2501 McGee, Mail Drop 215
Kansas City, MO 64141-6580

Or email us at:
booknotes@hallmark.com